EINE ALPENSINFONIE
AND
SYMPHONIA DOMESTICA

in Full Score

RICHARD STRAUSS

DOVER PUBLICATIONS, INC.
NEW YORK

Contents

This Dover edition, first published in 1993, is a republication of
the *Handpartitur* editions published by F. E. C. Leuckart, Leipzig, 1915 (*Eine Alpensinfonie, Op. 64*),
and Ed. Bote and G. Bock, Berlin, 1904 (*Symphonia domestica für grosses Orchester, Op. 53*).
The lists of instruments, dedications, notes and footnotes have been newly translated,
and explanatory notes and a Glossary of German terms have been added.

Manufactured in the United States of America
Dover Publications, Inc., 31 East 2nd Street,
Mineola, N.Y. 11501

Library of Congress Cataloging-in-Publication Data

Strauss, Richard, 1864–1949.
[Alpensinfonie]
Eine Alpensinfonie ; and, Symphonia domestica / Richard Strauss. —
In full score.
1 score.
Symphonic poems.
Reprint. Originally published: Leipzig : Leuckart, 1915 (1st work);
Berlin: Bote & Bock, 1904 (2nd work).
ISBN 0-486-27725-9
1. Symphonic poems—Scores. I. Strauss, Richard, 1864–1949.
Symphonia domestica. 1993. II. Title: Alpensinfonie. III. Title:
Symphonia domestica.
M1002.S91A4 1993   93-7493
CIP
M

Eine Alpensinfonie, Op. 64

Instrumentation

*2 Flutes—grosse Flöten (gr. Fl.)
2 Piccolos, doubling 3rd and 4th Flutes—kleine Flöten (kl. Fl.)
*2 Oboes—Hoboen (Hob.)
English Horn, doubling 3rd Oboe—englisch Horn (Engl. H.)
Heckelphone—Heckelphon (Heckelph.)
*Eb Clarinet—Es-Clarinette (Es-Clar.)
2 Bb Clarinets—B-Clarinetten (B-Clar.)
*C Clarinet, doubling Bass Clarinet in Bb—C-Clarinette (C-Clar.),
    Bassclarinette in B (Bassclar.)
3 Bassoons—Fagotte (Fag.)
Contrabassoon, doubling 4th Bassoon—Contrafagott (Contrafag.)

4 French Horns—Hörner
4 Tenor Tubas, doubling 5th, 6th, 7th and 8th Horns—Tenortuben
4 Trumpets—Trompeten (Trpt.)
4 Trombones—Posaunen (Pos.)
2 Tubas—Basstuben

2 Harps, doubled, if at all possible—Harfen
Organ—Orgel

Wind Machine—Windmaschine ⎫
Thunder Machine—Donnermaschine ⎪
Glockenspiel ⎪
Cymbals—Becken ⎪
Bass Drum—grosse Trommel ⎬ 3 Players
Side Drum—kleine Trommel ⎪
Triangle—Triangel ⎪
Cowbells—Herdengeläute ⎪
Gong—Tamtam ⎭
Celesta
Timpani (2 Players)—Pauken

At least:

18 1st Violins—I. Violinen (I. Viol.)
16 2nd Violins—II. Violinen (II. Viol.)
12 Violas—Bratschen (Br.)
10 Cellos—Violoncelle (Violonc.)
8 Double Basses—Contrabässe (C.-B.)

Offstage: 12 Horns, 2 Trumpets and 2 Trombones
    (if necessary, taken from the orchestra).

*In large orchestras, from rehearsal ⑨④ on, wherever the letter D appears in the 2 Flutes, Oboes, Eb and C Clarinet parts, these parts are to be doubled. (EDITOR'S NOTE: The doubling ceases where the letter E appears in these same parts.)

For the execution of the long ties (ligatures) in the winds, Samuel's Aerophon may be employed. (EDITOR'S NOTE: The Aerophon [OR Aerophor] was a bellows-like device, operated by foot and attached by a pipe to the mouthpieces of wind instruments, whereby a tone could be held, organ-like, indefinitely. The device was invented c. 1912 by the Belgian flutist Bernhard Samuel.)

Program of the Symphony

Nacht *Night* (p. 1)—Sonnenaufgang *Sunrise* (p. 10)—Der Anstieg *The ascent* (p. 16)—Eintritt in den Wald *Entry into the wood* (p. 24)—Wanderung neben dem Bache *A walk along the brook* (p. 37)—Am Wasserfall *At the waterfall* (p. 42)—Erscheinung *A vision* (p. 44)—Auf blumige Wiesen *Onto flowery meadows* (p. 53)—Auf der Alm *On the mountain pasture* (p. 55)—Durch Dickicht und Gestrüpp auf Irrwegen *Wrong turns through thicket and brush* (p. 63)—Auf dem Gletscher *On the glacier* (p. 74)—Gefahrvolle Augenblicke *Perilous moments* (p. 77)—Auf dem Gipfel *At the summit* (p. 79)—Vision *A vision* (p. 88)—Nebel steigen auf *The fog rises* (p. 99)—Die Sonne verdüstert sich allmählich *The sun is gradually obscured* (p. 101)—Elegie *Elegy* (p. 103)—Stille vor dem Sturm *Calm before the storm* (p. 105)—Gewitter und Sturm, Abstieg *Thunder and rainstorm, the descent* (p. 112)—Sonnenuntergang *Sunset* (p. 145)—Ausklang *Ending (of the day)* (p. 151)—Nacht *Night* (p. 159).

Dedicated with gratitude to Count Nicolaus Seebach
and the Royal Kapelle in Dresden

Eine Alpensinfonie

RICHARD STRAUSS, OP. 64

Nacht.
Lento.

1

Sonnenaufgang.
Festes Zeitmaß, mäßig langsam.

Der Anstieg.

Sehr lebhaft und energisch.

Eintritt in den Wald.

Wanderung neben dem Bache.

38 Allmählich bewegter.

Am Wasserfall.
Sehr lebhaft.

Auf blumige Wiesen.

Auf der Alm.

Festes, sehr lebhaftes Zeitmaß (un poco maestoso).

Auf dem Gipfel.

Etwas ruhiger.
Frei im Vortrag.

Vision.

Die Sonne verdüstert sich allmählich.

poco calando

Stille vor dem Sturm.

Gewitter und Sturm, Abstieg.

Schnell und heftig.

116   Eine Alpensinfonie

140   Eine Alpensinfonie

Sehr langsam.

Symphonia domestica, Op. 53

Instrumentation

Piccolo—kleine Flöte (kl. Flöte)
3 Flutes—grosse Flöten (gr. Flöten, gr. Fl.)
2 Oboes—Hoboen
Oboe d'amore
English Horn—englisch Horn (engl. Horn.)
Clarinet in D—D Clarinette (D Clar.)
Clarinet in A—A Clarinette (A Clar.)
2 Clarinets in B♭—B Clarinette (B Clar.)
Bass Clarinet in B♭—Bassclarinette (Bassclar.)
4 Bassoons—Fagotte (Fag.)
Contrabassoon—Contrafagott (Contrafag.)

4 Saxophones:
    Soprano in C—Sopran
    Alto in F—Alt
    Baritone in F—Baryton
    Bass in C—Bass
(Saxophones can be omitted, but only if absolutely necessary.)

8 French Horns—Hörner (Hörn.)
4 Trumpets—Trompeten (Tromp.)
3 Trombones—Posaunen (Pos.)
Bass Tuba—Basstuba (Tuba.)

4 Timpani—Pauken

Triangle—Triangel
Tambourine—Tamburin
Glockenspiel   } 2 Players
Cymbals—Becken
Bass Drum—grosse Trommel (gr. Trommel)

16 1st Violins   } Violinen (Viol.)
16 2nd Violins
12 Violas—Bratschen
10 Cellos—Celli (Violonc.)
8 Basses—Bässe (Contrab.)

2 Harps—Harfen

Symphonia domestica

RICHARD STRAUSS, OP. 53

★) Wenn die Pauke nicht genau auf die Höhe des obern Fis zu bringen, dann die Stelle ganz weglassen!
★) If the timpani is not precise in producing the high F-sharp, then omit the entire passage!

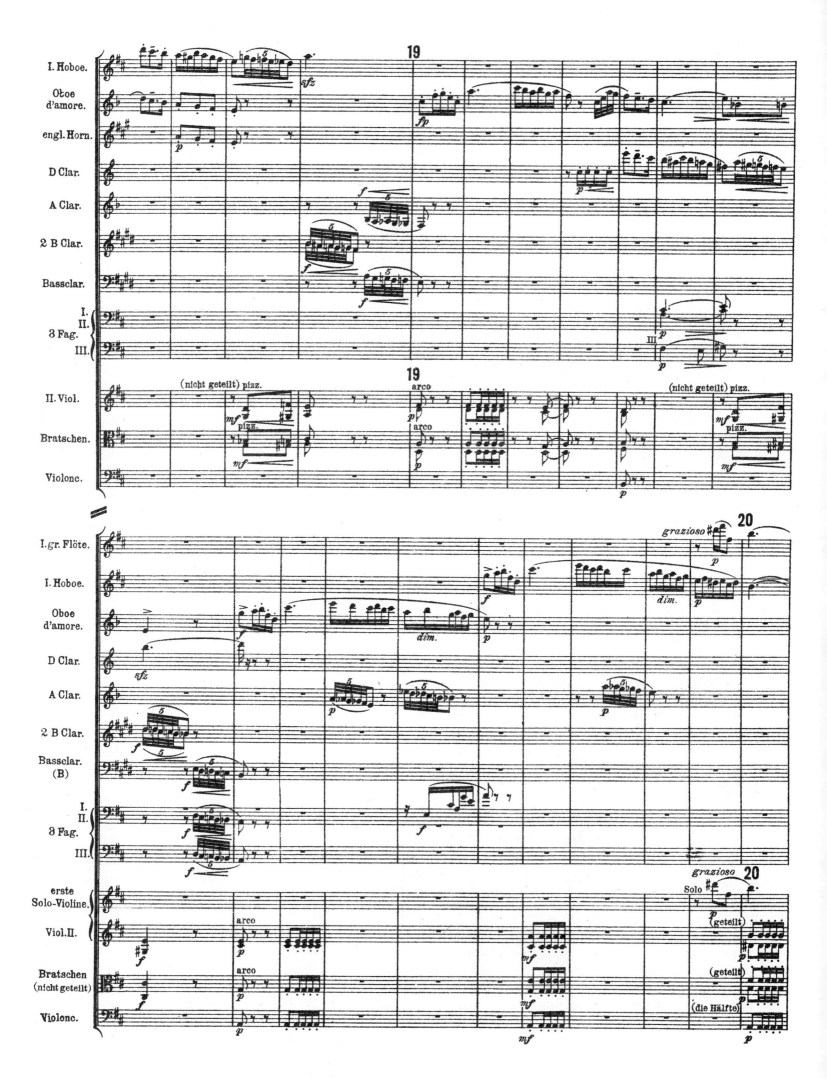

★) Diese kleinen Tempobezeichnungen sind stets nur als unbedeutende Modifikationen desselben Zeitmasses aufzufassen („sempre quasi l'istesso tempo")
★) These small tempo markings are always to be understood as only the slightest modifications to the established tempo (Sempre quasi l'istesso tempo).

*)die beiden Clarinetten stets in gleicher Stärke.

★) Both clarinets always with the same power.

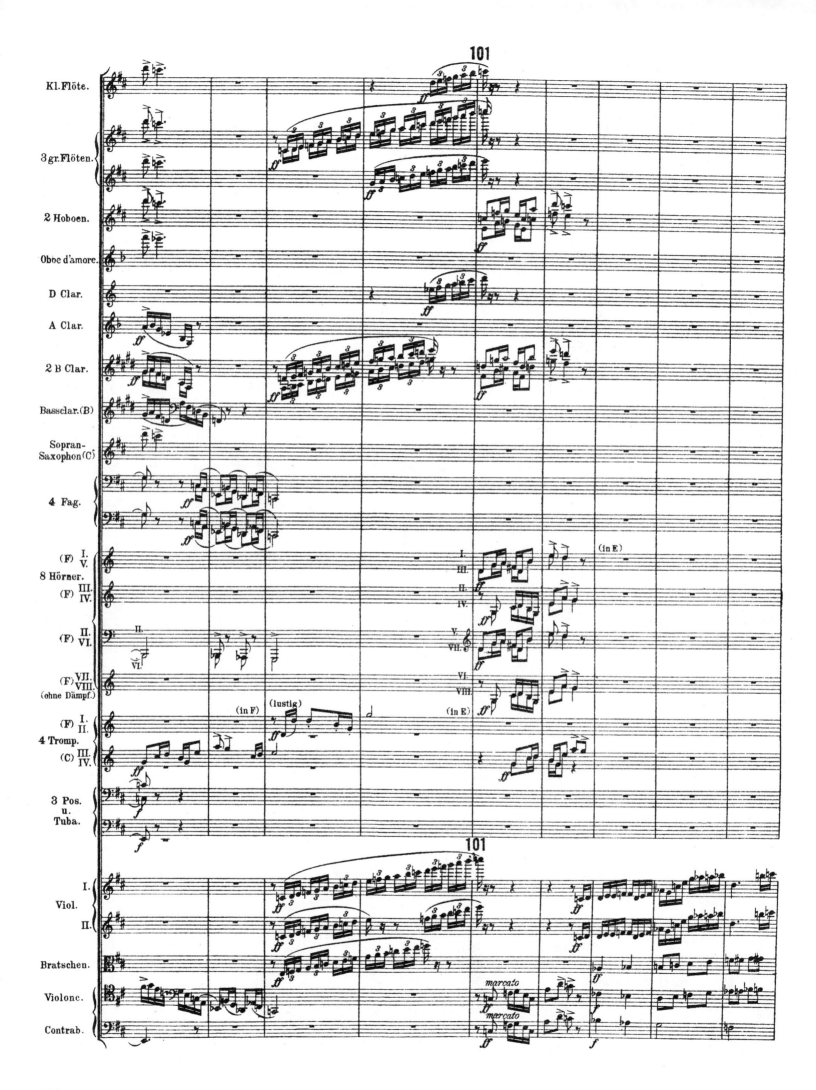

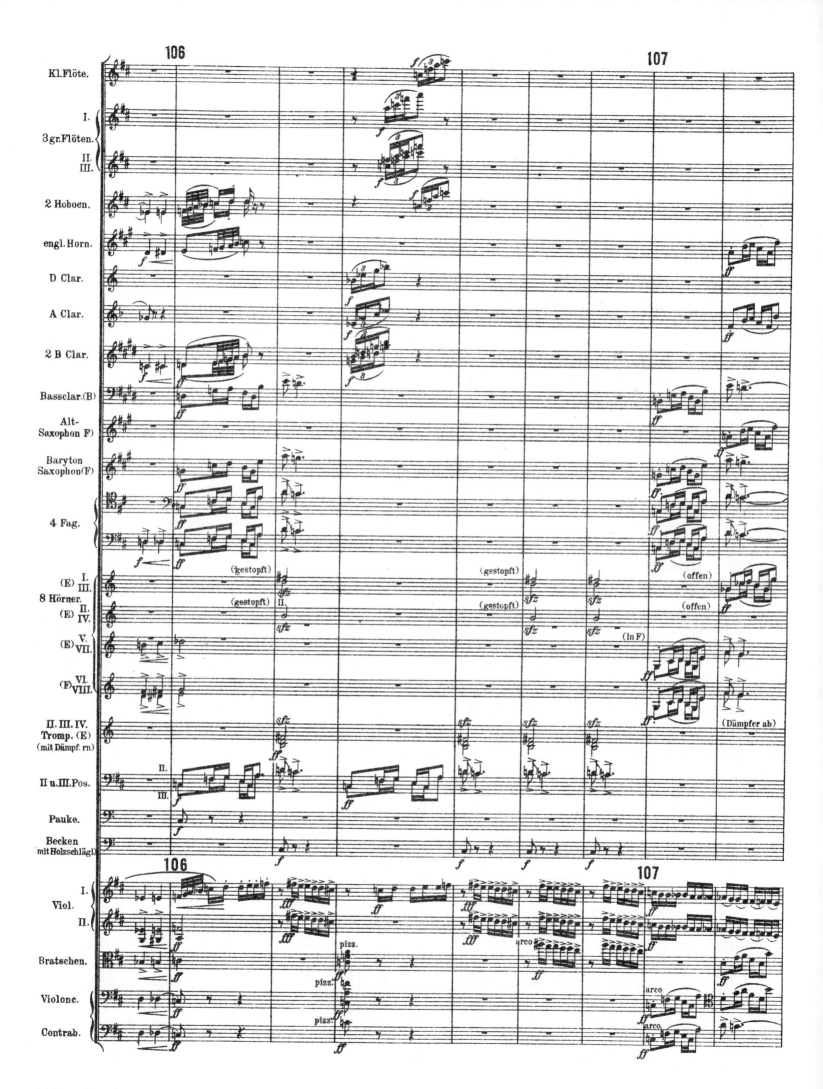

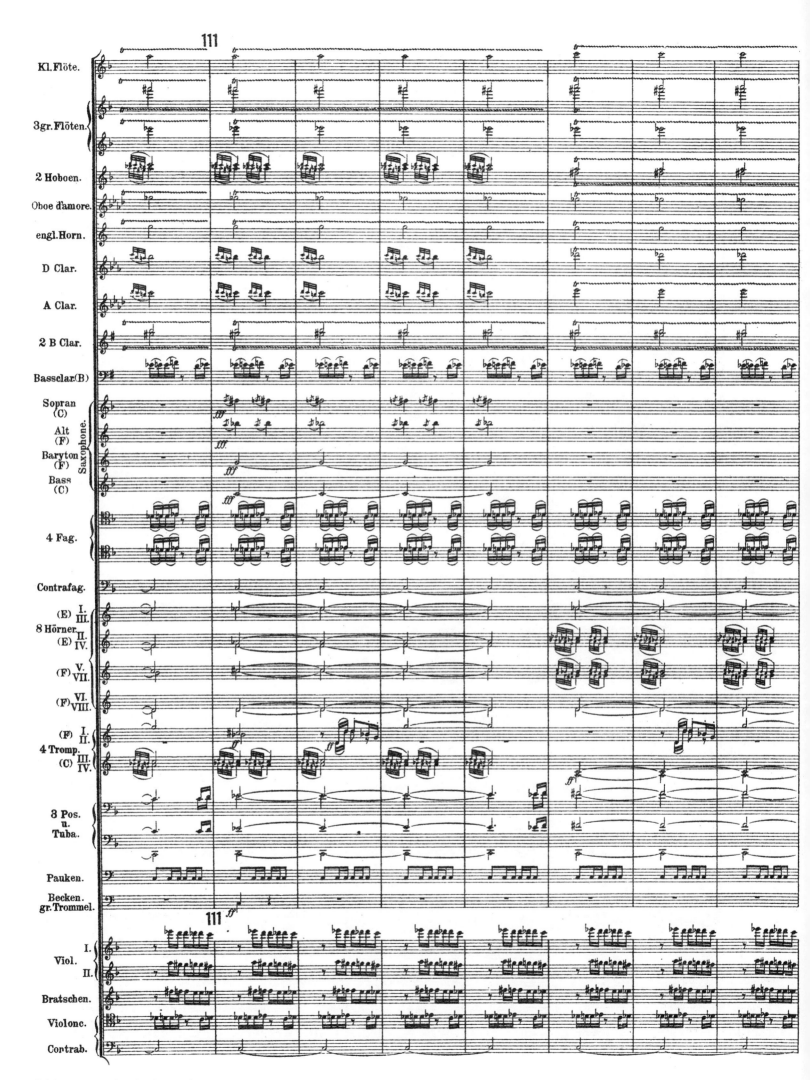

*) ⌢ 5 volle Takte lang.

★) ⌢ 5 full measures long.

Glossary of German Words and Phrases

ab, off, away
abnehmen, take away, remove
Achtel, eighth note
alle, all (tutti)
allein, solo, alone
allmählich, allmählig, gradually
als vorher, than before
am, at the
Anfangs, beginning, at first
ausdrucksvoll(er), (more) expressive
ausklingen lassen, let ring
äusserst, extremely

beginnen, begin
begleitend, accompanying
behaglich, comfortable, cozy
beide, both
beruhigen, become calmer
beschleunigen, accelerate
bewegt(er), lively (livelier)
breit(e), broad
breitem Strich, broad bowstrokes

Dämpfer(n), mutes
Dasselbe, the same
deutlicher, clearer
die Onkels, the uncles
die Tanten, the aunts
doch, so, thus
Doppelfuge, double fugue
doppelgriff, double stop
drängend, pressing ahead
drei-taktig, three-measure phrase
dreifach, (divided in) three parts

einfach, simple, plain, single
energisch, energetic
erste(s), first, original
Es, E-flat
etwas, somewhat

feierlich, solemnly
Fest(es), firm, solid
feurig, fiery, passionate
Flageolett, harmonic
Flatterzunge, fluttertongue
fliessend, flowing
Frei im Vortrag, free in execution (not strictly in tempo)
frisch, brisk
frisch vorwärts, moving briskly forwards
Frosch, frog
früheres, earlier, former

G-saite, G string
ganz, complete, full, very
"Ganz der Papa!", "Just like Father!"
"Ganz die Mama!", "Just like Mother!"
gefühlvoll, expressive, sentimental
gehalten, hold back
gemächlich, easy-going, gently
geschmeidig, supple, flexible
gestopft, stopped
geteilt, divided
getragen, solemn
gewöhnlich, ordinary
gleichmässig, equal

Hälfte, half
heftig, intense, impetuous
hervortretend, prominent
hinter der Scene, behind the scene (offstage)
Holzschlägel(n), wood stick(s)

immer, always
Immer im Charakter heftigen Drängens, Always impetuous and urgent (stringendo)
in 2 Hälften, in two halves
in sanfter Extase, in gentle ecstacy
innig, heartfelt

Jagdhörner von ferne, Hunting horns from afar

kurz, short

lang, long
langsam(er), slow(er)
lebhaft(er), lively (livelier)
leicht, light
leise, soft
lustig, jovial, merry

mässig, moderately
matt, languid, insipid, weary
mit, with
mit grosser Bravour, with much bravura
munter, cheerful
mürrisch, surly, irritable

nicht, not
nicht harpeggiert, not arpeggiated
noch, again, still

ohne, without

Paukenschlägeln, timpani sticks
plötzlich, suddenly
Pult(e), desk(s), stand(s)

ruhig(er), calm(er)

sanft, gentle
schnell, fast
schwächer, duller, lower
Schwammschlägeln, sponge-headed sticks
schwer, heavy
schwungvoll, spirited, enthusiastic
sehr, very
singend, in a singing manner, cantabile
springenden Bogen, bouncing bows (spiccato)
stark, strong
stärker, stronger, more vigorous
stärker einsetzen, begin more vigorously

träumerisch, dreamily
trotzig, obstinate, defiant

übrigen, others
und stets gut . . ., and constantly very . . .
unruhig, agitated, restless

verschwindend, disappearing, fading away
vierfach, (divided in) four voices
Viertel, quarter note
voll, full
volles Werk, full organ
von allen die Hälfte, half the total (number of)

weg, away
weich (gestrichen), smooth (bowing)
wenig, little
weniger, less
wie von Ferne, as if from afar
wieder, again
Wiegenlied, cradle song, lullaby

zart, smooth, legato
zärtlich, tenderly, affectionately
Zeitmass, tempo
ziemlich, reasonably
zornig, angry
zusammen, together
zwei-taktig, two-measure phrase
zweite, second

2-, 3-, 4-tactig, 2-, 3-, 4-measure phrases
3-, 4-, 5-fach, 3, 4, 5 parts